SAGGY BOOBS, STRETCH MARKS & SADDLEBAGS

By Birdie Chesson

Miss Birdie's Books, Inc.
New York

ISBN:
978-0-692-46555-4
Copyright 2014 by Birdie Chesson

TABLE OF CONTENTS

This book is dedicated to You.

FOREWORD

This book is a long time coming. We all know that sometimes things don't come together the way you want, *how* you want or *when* you want them to happen. Life is so unpredictable and so many things "happen" that you forget what you really wanted.

This book is like a love song that I've had in my heart for so long that I just couldn't put together to say the right words. I didn't want it to just be words. I wanted what I said to you to mean something. Truth is, it took me years to release this book because I've rewritten it several times.

As time moved on and my life unfolded more and more, everything that I wanted to tell you about wasn't my life anymore. I wanted to be totally transparent as possible, but now I realize the flaw in that thinking: Life constantly unfolds and my story will never be done. So I had to put the bookmark in at some point until I was ready to resume telling you more at another time.

Sometimes we go back in time to state how far we have come. I don't recommend revisiting the past frequently because life only moves forward, but my heart told me that this was a story that you needed to know so that you know where I'm coming from when I talk to you. Those who had followed me from the beginning know how I feel about you: I love you and I want you to do great in life.

Yes, you. I pride myself on being transparent and whether or not you love me back; all I want is for my life to be an example on how a regular everyday person can make a difference. No matter how stuck we may feel about it, life is great and everyone deserves to have a great life.

But I got in my own way for a long time.

I've had songs to sing ever since I could remember. People couldn't get me to shut up as a child. I had never even had a singing lesson. I was born and POW! I could sing. I sang professionally from the age of 15, doing vocal arrangements in studios, singing in clubs and private venues. My singing career was going comfortably well until I got pregnant at 26.

After that, I stopped singing altogether. I never understood the real reason why. Years later, when I was taking my son to school, as usual my son slept like he always did during our 2-hour commute. But on *this* day, when we got off of our bus, he started moving slowly and almost lethargic by the time we got to school.

When I took off his coat, he felt warm. So I took him to the school nurse so that she could take his temperature. A woman looked up and smiled at me. She wasn't the *regular* school nurse. But *this* woman was here on *this* day.

As she sat my son on the chair, she said,

"You look familiar."

I rolled my eyes, "I get that a lot. I have a familiar face."

"No, I've seen you before. Did you sing at BB Kings at Times Square before?"

WHOA! My antennas went up and I was dumbfounded. I've never been "a well-known name" in the music industry. But here I was, a *someone* to someone else.

Yes. I continued.

Her eyes lit up. "Well, what are you doing now?" I pointed to my son and gave the dumbest and weakest grin I could muster. "Motherhood. You know how it is."

She said, "No. I don't know how that is. Being a mom should never stop you from being who you are. You're hiding and that's a sin."

A SIN? Wait a minute, it's 8:30am in the morning, I think my son has a fever and as you take his temperature, you're lecturing me on my life's mission? I laughed it off though. I took it as her being an older woman who meant well.

"A sinner? That's big," I replied.

She continued, "What I mean is, God gave you a gift. Why are you hiding it?"

Now, this isn't a "religious book" and I hadn't cracked open a Bible in years but I knew she was talking about: Matthew 25: 14-30 *The Parable of the Talents.*

To make a long parable short, instead of using the talents "The Master" gave me, I, like the worthless servant, hid the talent in the ground and didn't make it work.

She stopped me in my tracks. In an instant, I was questioning everything I had done in my life since I had my son. At the time, he was 6 and here I was, still hiding behind that belly from years ago.

"I remember you like it was yesterday and I really enjoyed your voice. You deserve to be heard again. You're very gifted."

"Thank you. I'll think about it."

I took my 101-fever-having son home and I never saw that nurse ever again. It was a kick in the pants. But I still hesitated. Now even several years after that, here I am.

Your voice is a muscle. If you're not singing, your voice gets weak and if you don't sing at all, you lose your song. Sooner or later, your voice is gone.

I now remember how I feel when I get behind the mic, all of my fear and hesitation disappears and I become fearless. I love to sing.

After realizing that I had been the one holding myself back all of these years, I've gotten to the point now where I couldn't shut up all over again and why I stopped didn't matter anymore. It became, "When am I going to start again?"

Now is a good time. So here's my song.

CHAPTER ONE :

SAGGY BUSINESS

Why does it seem like there's that one day when you look in the mirror and you see that time has passed you by and life has beat the hell out of you?

It may be your birthday or even when the new year comes along and it's self-evaluation time *again*. Either way, you're standing there asking yourself, am I where I said I was going to be at this age/stage in my life?

For the fortunate ones, they are right there. They've accomplished all that they've set out to conquer and that's great for them. Then it's the rest of us that *another* year has passed us by and not much has changed. Your stomach sinks and your brain gets sluggish. So you intend to do better, but within months you're back in the same place.

First, I d like to say that I've been there a lot of times. Different stages in my life have brought me back and forth.

I'd be having a great few years, then something would happen and BOOM! I'm knocked on my butt and I'm worst off and/or having to begin again.

That's how this book started for me. I had been having a string of negatives. My business failed. Lost a long-time friend. Dead relationship. My son was sick, I was sick and I was tired. I wanted to give up. I was a single mom, which isn't unique; but everything was about my son and all I thought about was getting him the best care he needed. I was a robot, stuck in function mode.

Every year, I started out with zest and knew what I was going to do. A plan for greatness. So, to me, every year, I was off to a great start. It was going to be *my* year!

In 2008, I had come into a nice sum of

money from a work accident settlement. With the money, I took my family on vacation and invested in a video gaming lounge with a long-time friend of mine, Jason.

I had started my media company, The LOOK! Network, Inc. that my younger brother was videotaping events and music videos for. I'd edit the film and post them online. He'd get paid for the filming. I would get paid for editing.

The online posting got us more clients. We met a lot of colorful individuals to say the least, but it was fun. My brother was out and about with the who's who of New York while filming and I was at home, watching the tapes and living vicariously through him. So after I'd give the videos back to the clients, I was still in my apartment in Far Rockaway with my son but no real *life* of my own.

My son and I would commute two hours everyday to his school and during those 6 hours, I'd set up my portable business wherever the Wi- Fi was and I'd wait it out. Most days were productive but there were days where I'd literally be twiddling my thumbs.

At the time, my son's father and I were not on the best terms and I was pretty much on my own with Bam. In the creative industries, a lot of entrepreneurs and coaching clients work day jobs,

so me having flexible hours was needed because an event, job or opportunity can happen at any time. So if I had a meeting with a client after he got out of school, I either had to bring him, scramble to find a sitter or make some other excuse to have the client see me during an awkward time. I missed a lot of money and opportunities due to my inflexibility with time.

I had invested an initial $12,000 in Jason and I's video gaming lounge. He already had the space, which was next to 3 area schools and 3 train stations; with a main hospital off of Broadway and the West Side and Henry Hudson Highways, both close to the George

Washington Bridge. Needless to say, it was definitely a great demographic opportunity in New York.

Jason had the big screen TV's and I bought the gaming systems and games. I went to IKEA and bought 8 couches and with my electrician friends, we were about to wire everything up. It was an exciting time and we were going to capitalize on this great opportunity.

Jason and I were friends from when I first started to date Doug, my son's father, when we used to support Jason as a rapper. We went to his shows, gave out flyers that promoted him and his events. Years later, Jason started an online cable social network and when he told me about it, I saw the opportunity for my brother and our company, The LOOK! Network, Inc. to the next level.

We would take the footage that my brother taped and put it on our own channel, Channel 30. It was a great opportunity and soon we'd be making money through ads.

Programming the channel for 24/7/365 footage, with different shows and movies was tough, but it kept us busy and gave our business purpose and a vehicle to take us to the next level.

As for the gaming lounge, I was hiring people and was very excited because of the earning potential. I had my whole family involved in the process.

One day, I showed up to the property to take measurements and to see what else we would need to wire everything up with what we had, but I was locked out. Jason's mother told me that he went to Peru and other places to promote the network and decided to rent the space to someone else.

I was hurt and angry. Why would he do this? Why would he lock me out of *our* investment? And to make things worse, with no contact with Jason, we lost our channel on the network when everything went south. I was able to get the gaming systems back but he kept everything else, including my initial $12,000 investment in the lounge and additional money with the furniture. After not being able to reach him, I went to court and sued my friend. It was hard because it was the end of a friendship.

We lost two huge parts of what my brother and me built around the channel and the lounge,not to mention losing the investments. After all was said and done, I didn't have any money left from my settlement. Those losses and the betrayal of my friend rattled me to my soul.

With nowhere to showcase the footage my brother was shooting, his clients opted to use other media platforms to showcase their work. The LOOK! Network, Inc. was on ice and my brother found a day job to take care for himself and his responsibilities.

I settled into a rut. I was feeling sorry for myself, running around in my mind as to what I did wrong or how I could've done things differently. I was borderline obsessed, grasping at straws trying to figure out how to make money.

I was back to small editing jobs that did just enough business as well as some video editing to keep food on the table and participate in minimal activities.

That was our life for 5 years. I was bored, restless and sad. I was in my early thirties but I didn't know where to start anymore. My singing life had dried up; the live band that I sang with previously had disbanded and was doing other things. I had no more contacts with the producers I had worked with in the past.

So after thinking of my *"what next?"* I leaned back on what I was good at, my writing. In the 90's, I had started writing children's books but when I'd send queries to publishers, all I got were rejection letters. When you get a rejection letter, they never say why. They just say no.

So at first, I thought it was me. Why didn't they like me?

Then I learned about getting an agent but nothing for me there either. Here I was, with a ton of stories that I wanted to share with families, and I felt silenced. Until I thought, *"Why not own my own contributions and keep everything?"*

That's when I officially started my business: Miss Birdie's Books, Inc. I've always seen myself as a mogul of sorts, so it came to me that I could be the face of my own book publishing company. Problem was, I didn't know where to start. I didn't know any business owners at the time, let alone anyone in the book industry.

I didn't have money to invest in my business so I went to the public library and read books on self- publishing and went online to find ways to publish my books without paying upfront costs.

I needed a website for my books to have a home. I read books on coding and spent many nights creating a website. My first website was a mess but I was so proud of it because it was mine and the world could Yahoo Search or Google me and find me.

Looking for ways to make professional copies of my books, I found *Lulu* and *Createspace (Now KDP)*, an *Amazon company*. With them, I learned about covers and interiors, sizing and structure of books; as well as selling them. I couldn't even afford to buy my own books, let alone stockpile hundreds to sell on my own so those avenues were great options for me.

I was afraid that no one would like my books or even buy my books but all I knew was that I had to try. I had messages that applied to real life. In my past life as a nanny and caregiver, I knew that the stories needed to be told. So I told the stories.

Crickets. No one knew about me to buy the books so they sat on my website and on Amazon for years, collecting dust. But I felt accomplished as a published author. It definitely wasn't paying the bills but it was all I had at the time.

In all those years of building my businesses,

one of my favorite sayings is, "No one sees you if you're winking in the dark." The part of the business mindset that I was missing was *me*.

Truth was, I was still afraid to truly put myself out there so I didn't promote myself.

What if people didn't like me? Maybe the publishing houses were right about my work and I wasn't good enough. The books were just existing, like I was. "If you build it, they will come", only applies to baseball fields, but you can't build a business like that. I had to take a chance on myself and show the world who I was and why what I said mattered. But I wasn't ready yet.

I will repeat this throughout this book because it will always apply: There's no guarantee that anyone will like you and what you have to offer, but you have to gamble on yourself, you never know what it'll be and when it will pay off. Release the work and keep moving forward.

In all of the creations that I made after the

business debacle with Jason, I'm not even sure what held me back at the time. All I knew was that I still felt stuck.

CHAPTER TWO:

SAGGY FAMILY

Before all of the business stuff hit the fan, I was in a loving relationship with my son's father. Although the everyday ins and outs of the day gave us occasional stress, we still had each other and were making it all work smoothly. Our son was a beautiful, happy and overall healthy child. Together, we made a great family.

But we only *appeared* to have it together, which was the reason our split was so shocking to others. The illusion of us was so deceptive. Our family chemistry was so "on" all of the time that even we didn't know that there was anything wrong until it fell apart and when it ended, it was ugly.

In the beginning, everything with us just flowed. With the exception of family obligations, we were pretty carefree. We had our own separate lives but we were very supportive of each other.

He would go to every one of my shows when I'd perform and be my date to every movie premiere red carpet event I was invited to.

When he returned to college, I cosigned on the loans. To me, this was *us* building a future and we were a team.

Life was a well-oiled machine. So when I found out that I was pregnant, I was scared but I was secure in knowing that we had each other.

In fact, when I told him the news, he asked, "Do you trust me?" I said yes. He grabbed my hand and we walked to the Hudson River and he surprised me with a kayaking lesson. It was his plan for us for the day and although the news made him pause, he was happy.

But I was the one that was so unsure. Our lives were about to change in a big way and I was scared. Every time I would tell him how I was feeling, he'd be so attentive and encouraging. Nightclubs were still not a place for a pregnant woman or a baby, so we agreed that I wouldn't sing in clubs anymore and I didn't know where else I could sing. So I stopped singing. I felt like my life was on a hard halt.

Overall, my pregnancy was great. No real weight gain, no morning sickness. I craved pickles with garlic onion potato chips and Doug was armed with my craving requirements every time he came home from work.

Two months into my pregnancy, there was a family emergency and my entire immediate family ended up staying at our house. It was supposed to be temporary but 3 weeks turned into 8 months and it felt like an eternity.

With six adults in a studio apartment, Doug started coming home later and later, because he felt that there was no privacy at home. He picked up more shifts at work and even started staying at his mother's house because it was closer to his job. Hell, it was so crowded that I didn't want to be home either. I was jealous that he felt able to opt out of coming home.

By the time I finally put my foot down and made my family leave, Doug and I were already ripping at the seams. I felt neglected and left behind, so did he. We loved each other but I started to feel that he was somewhere else. He came home because there was no reason not to come home anymore. We started our old patterns again but we felt apart. Knowing that our lives were about to change added to the complexity of our distant energy.

Meanwhile, we rejoiced at every appointment, took Lamaze and parenting classes. We were getting ready for baby life and did small things to keep up our spirits, such as date nights and weekend getaways but internally, we had fracture.

Bam didn't turn and after scheduling a cesarean, our Bam had other plans and decided on coming the night before. After the rush to the hospital, which was an event in itself, we were there and ready for baby.

Doug held my hand as the doctor cut me open and pulled our baby out of me. I cried as I felt him leave my body and I heard him cry. Our lives were so different in that moment. All that mattered was Bam, Doug and I.

On the day that we brought our son home, we had a mini party with family and friends in attendance. Later, Doug took his mother home. After a few hours, everyone left. But Doug didn't come back home that night.

I was still in pain from the cesarean and couldn't even pull our Murphy bed down. I was so tired and Bam wouldn't stop crying. I would be feeding him and he'd still be crying. I knew he was hungry but he wasn't eating. I was in so much pain and by 3 a.m., Doug's phone went straight to voicemail.

At 5am, I called my mother and she came to get me and Bam. I was so tired, so hurt, so alone and in shock. When he finally called back around noon, he said that he fell asleep on the couch at his mother's and then his phone died. I was so hurt and angry that he had left me and the baby with no help, knowing the condition that I was in. I couldn't even begin to conceive why he wouldn't come back home to us immediately. But there I was, in my mother's house with a screaming newborn.

After me not answering my phone, Doug came home to find that I wasn't there. He called my mother and got a good tongue-lashing. He came later that evening to take me and Bam home.

On top of the tension between Doug and I, when feeding, Bam would only drink an ounce or two of his bottle and would fall asleep. I was worried because he wasn't really eating. When he was born, the nurse in the hospital said that he had a "slow suck". It was odd but we didn't think anything was wrong until we returned to the doctor for his first visit.

The nurse there discovered that Bam had a cleft palate and was indeed starving. Being that I have a seizure disorder, I knew that there was a 1-3% chance of a birth defect but when you take medication to live, you never realistically think about the real life side effects until you see the damage up close and personal.

He couldn't suck, which was why he couldn't drink without getting tired and falling asleep. He did all of that work and could only eat a little food. My poor baby was exhausted and starving.

That day, we had an emergency appointment with the craniofacial team at now NorthWell Hospital, where a great nurse was waiting and had these special Haberman nipples that we could actually pump the milk into our son's mouth. We had to be on rhythm with him. So as he'd swallow, we'd pump. I was so happy when my son actually finished a bottle. He grew, got nice and chunky.

Although we had found a solution for Bam, I was still in bad shape. It didn't help that I had sunk into postpartum depression.

Conflicted with my emotions, I felt selfish because I was sad all of the time, wanting to get out but feeling stuck and so confined in my own life. I wanted to live but I didn't have a life. Even worse, I felt like Doug and I were moving further apart.

There were subtle hints that he was cheating on me. I kept going back in my mind when he had told me that we'd be a team as a family and by that time, I felt like he lied to me. He was always in the wind and I was always alone with the baby, with no real outlet of my own.

On top of all of the angst and loneliness that I was feeling about Doug and I, my father was in a hospice with terminal cancer. When I poured my heart out to my dad about my suspicions, he said, "Doug is just scared. Keep the family together."

I remember asking him, "But what about me, Daddy? Don't I deserve more?"He said, "He'll come around. Don't leave him; he'll be lost without you. It's just a phase."

Coming from him, a man dying alone in the hospital, his words weighed a ton on my heart. That day, I took my baby home and cried. That night was another night that Doug did not come home at all. He'd go to work early, come home late, if he came home at all.

After my maternity leave, I finally went back to work. I still went to school, got my baby and came home lonely. The cycle was the same day in and day out. The push/pull of us was tedious and it slowly destroyed me.

My dad seemed to be the biggest champion for our relationship. So when I lost him, I expected Doug to upset about it. But Doug didn't come home the night he died and didn't go to his funeral.

I was angry, hurt and didn't care that I

didn't make it easy for him to be home now. Between the prank calls and messages women were leaving, I knew that he was blatantly cheating.

But I was so jaded by this point that when he was home, you could cut the tension with a knife. I wanted him to stop the torture and choose to finally leave us but he didn't get the telepathic message. I didn't have the heart to make him go. So we slowly tore each other apart. I already felt like a single mother because I was always alone with our son.

Bam was 2 years old and was about to have cleft repair surgery. I knew that after surgery, there would be a long road of recovery for him, full of therapies and specialists. Compounded with the injuries I accumulated at the job, the union proposed that I cash out my future value in a lump settlement. So I made the hard decision to leave my career as an electrician to take care of my baby full time.

By this time, Doug was coming home less

and less. He'd get off of work on a Friday and we wouldn't see him until Sunday morning.I ignored what Doug was doing because I was in a fog. So much was going on and Doug and I felt completely broken.

After Bam s surgery, he was on a strict pureed food diet and was very cooperative for a 2 year old. Imagine pureed spaghetti, veggies or even fried chicken! Going back to baby food wasn't easy but Bam is the best.

After a month, when Bam was able to eat solid foods again, Doug and I had a mini party for him; complete with friends, cake and actual pizza.

After everyone left, while cleaning up, we all had a food fight. We laughed and played and even Bam got a few digs in. That night, after Bam went to sleep, Doug rubbed my feet and we made love like we hadn't in years. I melted in his arms and went to sleep.

In the middle of the night, he started

grumbling and was talking in his sleep. I heard him say, "She's pregnant." I shot up quickly, started hitting him to wake up and shouted questions. Still groggy, he tearfully confessed. I was in shock.

He told me that he wanted to be caught and held accountable but my pretending that I didn't know made it seem ok, that I let him do it, so he took it as permission and kept cheating. "WHAT?"

Yes, he actually said it. He blamed me for the outcomes of his cheating. I was shocked by his audacity.

In hindsight, it wasn't a real surprise. But I was blindsided with the reality of the truth. I did know about her for months. It was crazy but again, I acted like if I treated her like she didn't exist like she'd go away. I felt physically sick. I didn't want to stand for this anymore.

So after he left for work, I changed the locks, packed his clothes, and brought them to his mother's house. I hid out at my mother's house and didn't answer his calls. I was so hurt but I couldn't stand for this and I didn't know what else to do.

We didn't speak for weeks and Bam was constantly asking for his father. It was at a family event that we both showed up to that Bam finally saw his father. He was so happy but I was still heartbroken. We kept up some semblance of a facade but our extended family wasn't fooled.

They told Doug to fix his family. After the party, he walked us to the train in silence and we parted ways.

A few days later, he showed up with a duffel bag and asked to stay. We spoke honestly and put everything on the table. We both agreed that we wanted to make our family work. We had that indoctrinated in us because that's what our own parents did amidst their own infidelities and internal fighting. I was still hurt but I knew that I wasn't done with us. I really thought that we could turn us around. So I told him that he could come back but he had to stay on the couch.

He would have to be consistently vested at working on our family and subsequently make his way back to our bed.

He went to work at 6pm and came home at exactly 1:45am and if he was running late, he called. I was happy that he was making the effort to bring us back on track. We were doing better but the months before his baby would be born felt like an eternity.

The days before the other woman's due date, we spent together. We knew that life wouldn't be the same. I didn't know what to feel. On the day of her baby shower, I called her and wished her the best. I can't explain why I did it.

I know that it was mind blowing to her, but I didn't care. I really meant her well and wanted to let go of the pain I felt. I was trying to be strong and accept what was happening. I guess I wanted her to know I was fine. But I wasn't.

The night she went into labor, Doug and I

were at a party. He was glued to my side all night. We took pictures. Our family was so happy to see us together. But I had a feeling of doom. Our family dynamic was about to change and I wasn't ready. The night was over and it was early morning now. Doug wanted to stay with me but I knew that him being there for his son's birth was more important than any feeling that I felt, no matter how selfish I wanted to feel at the time. So I encouraged him to go to the hospital to be by her side.

I stayed in the bed all day, by the phone. Doug called me with the blow-by-blow news. I was destroyed by it all, but I remained supportive to Doug. Sixteen hours later, Doug was a father again. I was devastated.

He tried to be supportive to the mother but a few hours after the baby's birth, he rushed home to be with Bam and me.

She was probably upset by his abandonment, but I didn't feel sorry for her at all. I was bitter. Doug tried to placate me by deserting her. We had our own son. He poured extra energy into Bam. He was on the verge of pretending that his other child did not exist.

So did I.

We sunk head first into more family activities. Going back on family vacations, throwing our famous parties again. Even though we were doing greater as a couple than ever, I saw a sadness in Doug.

He was trapped. Here he had a family that he finally got back, but now there was a cloud of guilt hovering over him.

I believe that he thought that being only with us was the right thing to do. But he was divided. He didn't want to hurt me anymore, so he was making a choice to stay away. Seeing how miserable he was, I encouraged Doug to see his infant son. So every other weekend, he'd see his son.

One Saturday, after visiting his son, he came home late. While I was doing laundry, he emptied his pockets on the kitchen table to put his pants in the wash. Movie tickets, restaurant receipts were there on the table. If this was a newborn child, why are you going to the movies, why are you going to restaurants the baby can't even eat in?

I understand maintaining camaraderie with your child's mother and not making a tricky situation worse, but I was no fool. These were dates. When I approached him with what I found, I remember how nonchalant he was in his response. "But you got *me*."

He sat smug on the couch. I followed in disgust. "I got you? What did I do to deserve *you*?" In that moment, I saw that he thought that the women in his life were competing in a sick contest and he was the prize. I was completely dumbfounded. The total understatement was that this situation was completely out of hand. I told him that if "this" was what I won, I didn't want him anymore.

When he left to go to work, I started to dig. I wanted to know everything. I went through bank statements, phone messages and gifts.

That day, I found out that his other son s mother wasn't the only one; there were other women now.

When I found the proof, my heart stopped. He was completely out of hand. It was like he was punishing me for not punishing him. But I didn't know what to do. I was devastated and confused but I couldn't ignore it. I was fighting the wrong fight. What was I doing? Why was I still in this? There shame in being alone after being together for so long. Like I failed. At the time, I felt like needed to belong to someone, even if it was a lie.

Overall, I knew that I was losing what we built. No one likes to lose after such an investment in time and love. I constantly thought about what my father said and when I made up my mind,by this point, I wanted our family to work so badly that I was reduced to a woman who was waiting for a life I thought I deserved with a man that didn't deserve it. He was out doing what he wanted and I was waiting for him to come around.

We always "got along" because we had a natural rapport that put others at ease, even when we were at our worst.

But being together made us both unhappy now.

Whenever he'd leave the house, I was actually relieved. While he was gone, life with Bam and I was laid back. But when Doug came home, it felt like he disrupted the order of things and he felt it. This was *our* home now, just me and Bam.

Doug was almost an unwanted guest out of place whenever he came home. I didn't even let him touch me anymore. There was no love, no sex, no us.

I decided that Doug had to go. Before, I felt lonely without him. Now I felt lonely *with* him. Now, looking back, after all this time maybe I was just comfortable with being uncomfortable. What kind of life is that?

My dad always told me that a man should always feel like a man, so as I went on in my mind, I actually thought that I took that away from him because I was too focused on Bam and his health issues. I was an independent businesswoman and didn't depend on Doug for anything. That I didn't make Doug feel like he should have as a man, so he found someone else that did.

Nope. I was not about to own that.

Remember: Whatever you put up with is exactly what you will have and I was tired of this life. No more wondering where he was, whom he was with, I didn't care anymore. I packed the rest of Doug's things and waited for him to come home. When he came in, I told Doug that he shouldn't come back for the last time. He said that he'd never forgive me for making him leave. He was upset that I gave up on us. The nerve!

Truth is, when you blame each other, you both give up your power to change. Once you realize that you've given away your power you can always make the decision to take it back. I needed peace in my heart.

Immediately, the weight of the burden was lifted from me. The next day, I took Bam to school as usual, but my head was held high and didn't pay any mind that it was a rainy day. I was free.

It made me sad that Doug and I were actually over but it was time to redefine a life with just me and Bam and that gave me hope.

School. Work. Life. Rinse and repeat, with before and now without Doug. It was business as usual.

I wanted to be best mother to our son, Bam. I had to be the best me.

So I chose me.

CHAPTER THREE

SAGGY MOMMY

On a rapidly sinking ship, a woman wearing a life jacket straps her young son into a life jacket and while holding him tightly, she jumps overboard. She quickly grabs her son and starts to swim away quickly.

As the boat sinks in the distance, she finally peeks her head above water. Seeing the debris and no rescue in sight, she looks into the sky. "Please help me." She whispers quietly. A tear rolls down her face, she smiles reassuringly to her son to calm his cries. "Are you OK?" Catching his breath, he nods his head.

Composing herself, she leans her head back while her son nervously holds her neck. "Keep holding on to me." She closes her eyes and allows herself to become weightless. She becomes her son's lifeboat and they float...

I had that dream. The woman was me, and

the boy was my son. It scared me. And it wasn't pretty.

So I moved on in my life, still with writing and editing. I was slowly building my momentum back up. I was still financially in a hole, digging myself out. But I was slowly seeing my way clear.

Every once in a while, Doug and I would have a disagreement when he wasn't picking Bam up or coming to see him but Doug's inconsistency didn't stop our flow. Bam and I had our own daily routine.

In 2011, Hurricane Irene was on its way and we had to evacuate the Rockaways. I was so scared because we were on our own. The city closed down the only hospital in Rockaway, Peninsula Hospital.

Mentioned in one of the town hall meetings, it was said, "Every 30 years, the Atlantic Ocean meets the Jamaica Bay." I was like, "WHAT?"

I looked up the town record and there it was in the 1970's, 5 feet high floods that covered over the entire Rockaway Peninsula. And in the 1930's before that. I'm thinking, "We re overdue for another catastrophe!"

Doug and I had settled there years before as a new beginning to start our own family. But since we didn't work out, me and Bam's everyday was in the city everyday and now the history of disasters, I knew that Bam and me definitely had to get out of the '*Rock*'.

Two months later, there was a winter storm coming with a coastal flood watch and I didn't want get stuck in Rockaway so we left and went to my sister's house. Bam had been having a series of fevers lately but Bam was his natural happy self with no other symptoms so I didn't see any cause for alarm, even after the school nurse sent him home.

This time, I had the Children's Tylenol in tow so we were on our way. Hours after I put Bam in bed, he started to snore really loud, but it was a sound I had never heard come from him. I checked on him and he was very hot. I went to take his *temperature,*

I must've scared him and he went into a violent seizure. He was at 104 degrees and my sister was packing the ice and stripping him naked to cool him off.

He went into 4 more seizures in 25 minutes.

It had just started snowing. I wrapped him in blankets, grabbed his limp body and jumped in the car. The hospital was ten minutes away and my sister got us there in two. I jumped out of the car hysterically and the nurse stopped me in my tracks. I said to her tearfully, "Please help my baby." She says, "Stop crying, child. Be strong. Your baby needs you to be strong." A calm rested over me as I handed over my son to the nurses to put him on the gurney. My sister called Doug and he answered. She told him where we were and he came as fast as he could.

Bam didn't have any more seizures but the doctor wanted to put him on medication to prevent more seizures. I wasn't about to let him be medicated if he didn't need to be, especially not knowing what caused it. I wanted answers. So I got a second opinion.

I found a notable pediatric neurologist, Dr. Kashyar Khodabaksh that was in Manhattan and although we'd have to travel 2 hours to see him, it was worth it.

With Bam having seizures, I had a sense of guilt and helplessness that I had never experienced before. I was so sad that the perfect munchkin that I had brought into the world was going through something so drastic and I couldn't help him. And with my own epileptic history, I felt like it was my fault.

When I told a friend of mine about everything, and how long it was taking for Bam to see all of these doctors and specialists, she told me that I can put in for emergency housing to get out of Rockaway and closer to a hospital for his care. I did that in January. I got a letter in April that we were accepted into New York City Housing Authority's Amsterdam Houses.

Now I will tell you, living in Manhattan has

always been one of my dreams and as much as it was public housing, it was across the street from Lincoln Center. LINCOLN CENTER!!!

I was nervous because it was very close to where Doug was now living but I thought it couldn't hurt for Bam to be closer to his father. I accepted the apartment and got ready to move right away.

His neurologist told me that his seizures are factor based. Upper Respiratory Infections obstruct his breathing which causes him to breath hard and his temperature goes up = fever based, and stress related."

What could he possible be stressed about? Then I remembered that he would complain that his mind was always racing, so I got him a notebook to relay all of these thoughts.

"Why do old people tell so many stories? Why do people that speak Spanish, talk so fast? Why does my teacher have so much hair in his ears?" There must have been page upon page of rambling

questions like that in his book. In the mind of a 9 year old that doesn't want to go to sleep, he thought of every trick in the book to stay up. Even if it was to write in that "Thought Book". All jokes aside, it seemed to relieve some of his stress and pressure.

Dropping Bam off at school one morning, as I walked down the driveway, I saw Doug peeking behind a car. A family member walked up to me, handing me an envelope. It was a petition for custody. I lost my mind. I cursed Doug up and down the street and when I was done screaming the truth, the family member looked at him really crazy and apologized to me for getting involved.

The truth was, Doug was always able to get Bam, and he just didn't come. He said that he wanted a specific time and day that we'd both honor. Not an unreasonable request but he often wanted Bam short notice and at times that we weren't available. I wanted regularity too but I never thought of taking Doug to court. But here we were.

After Bam's seizures, we had a degree of

civility between us that this blindside felt like a complete betrayal. So upset, I filed papers of my own for sole custody. We were feuding and it was ugly.

Everyone who knew us knew about it and was trying to stay neutral. We both wanted our sides to be heard and it alienated a lot of family, friends and every sympathetic ear. In hindsight, I regret dragging people into my hell. But I had already felt so alone in the saga between Doug and I that I wanted to let everyone know how much he hurt me.

In the end, I was awarded full custody. Doug and I agreed that he could have alternate weekends and agreed upon holidays and school vacations.

We were going to be active co-parents. I was so angry after the custody battle. But there was finality my anger. With each court date, I had experienced a mourning that I never had come to terms with before.

I was disappointed with Doug for trying to take Bam from me after all that he had done to wreck our family.

I was completely done with romanticizing or entertaining any future that could have existed between us in our more peaceful times. He hurt me for the last time.

I was absolutely done in my heart with Doug.

Most of all, I hated the custody battle because Bam was the boy that neither of us "owned" but was now almost reduced to property that "belonged" to either me or his father.

I hated how that made me feel. It was just my son and I for so long that *how dare* he come in and try to take him away from me. He didn't see that filing for custody leads to a perception that a mother is not taking care of her child.

I see now that all he wanted was an in, a chance to do better by Bam in his own way, but all he had to do was talk to me and stay consistent.

He got that chance. Now it has freed me in a way that I am grateful. My son needed his father. I always protected our son from things that could hurt him. Was I hurting him by fighting to prove I was the better parent? Perhaps.

I never spoke ill about his father to our son but the tension was so thick between us that my energy exuded hate for the man that I once loved dearly.

One thing I've learned is that happiness is simple. Happiness is not contingent on anything but you.

Every time I think about how hard things get to me, I'm the one that's ultimately in charge of my own future. We humans make it hard. We let our minds and lives become consumed with things that just take our focus away from what we are really supposed to be doing.

The mirror shows the unadulterated truth. It's *all* there. It's our perception of your reflection that skews the image you think you see.

I love what I see. Love the person I am to myself and my reflected public representation is on point.

Cool, refreshingly flawed, rational/irrational, enthusiastic and positive. It is very important to me how people view me. I'm a people person. A businesswoman. But it doesn't steer me, it's a natural progression.

I only worry about if I did my best job as Bam's Mama. I can mess up being Birdie, pick myself up, dust myself off but I can't mess up being Bam's Mama. Ever.

With children, good and bad, they are a mirror reflection of us. And my son was magnifying the worry, the stress that he felt in my company.

So what was I stressed about? How could I stop projecting that onto him?

I work at night after he sleeps. Any editing jobs, writing assignments, this book even, are all mostly done at night so that I don't have any disturbances.

Mom, can I have water? I'm hungry again. "Can I watch cartoons?" "What are you doing?" And he sits on my lap and wants me to hold him.

I love my son with all of my heart, and I miss him dearly when he and I are apart. I know there will be the days that I wish I heard the pitter-patter of teensy feet and he will grow out of wanting me to hold him (and I'll be heartbroken) but sometimes I really need to concentrate in order to bring home the bacon. Kids don't really understand that.

The stresses of deadlines, my own projects, raising my son alone were all taking a toll and I didn't realize it. Kids feel that and take it personally.

You don't want to give that to them. So sometimes, you stop to hold them and read stories and let them see what you're working on because he wants to be involved in the process. But there is never enough time in the day.

There's a saying, "Kids get their awesome from their mommies."

My son is a total mirror reflection of me, my face, personality, my charm, my strength, my creativity, my honesty, sense of self, my confidence, my generosity, my friendliness, my huge heart and capacity to love and wearing his heart on his sleeve, my rhythm (or lack there of) and my vision. But he also has my naiveté, the ability to be hurt easily, my short attention span, my clownish & silly ways.

I'm sure that there are other things that are great and also a total mess about me, but you can look at him, and he's all me.

As Bam's mom, I am supposed to give him the best tools possible to be the best him he can be as an adult. Let him go out into the world to make his own way with the experiences and pearls that I gave him.

I knew that I had to be more conscious of the life I was creating for him. I had to decide to be a better mom. How could I do that if I'd keep myself at the mercy of others? How could I do that if I was just reacting from what was happening to me instead of creating the life me and Bam deserved?

When you put up with bad behavior from others, it's like martyring yourself for the sake of being a saint and from the distance you're just a doormat. I said when you KEEP being the bigger person, it teaches the other person that that is how to treat you... How often do you keep standing in the line of fire and continue to get fired upon before you move?

In everything that I had been through, I realized that I needed to choose me. Choosing me, I chose *us*.

This sinking ship of uncertainty in this life, the leap of faith that everything will be ok; the floating with him trusting me is *our* journey together.

Tell me what I don't know...

You block your blessings by having people in your life that take away from you whether its energy, talent and time. You also block your blessings by staying too long in places that you are supposed to move away from.

The storms that I had been through had carried me to that point. Away from Jason, away from Doug and away from Rockaway.

By the way, if we hadn't left Far Rockaway when we did, we would've been stuck after Hurricane Sandy. We moved only 5 months previously.

Everything happens for a reason...

CHAPTER FOUR :

SAGGY THOUGHTS

Now living in Manhattan, I knew that I was in a geographical position where I could finally be more proactive and excited about my *own* future.

But admittedly, Miss Birdie's Books, Inc. was in shambles. I owed back taxes and although I had released several books and was still having book- coaching sessions, I was lost.

After dealing with so much and just going through the motions, I really floating aimlessly. Truth was, I did not know how I was going to be successful after inactivity in my business for so long.

So I dug my heels in and started to actively pursue clients and started to write more books. I paid off some of my fines and started to get back into the groove of things in business.

I was so proud of myself. I worked hard and my writing and editing business was doing good, but no matter how much I actually did now, it was overshadowed by the fact that I didn't get up and actually leave the house, sit at a desk in some other building and what I was doing now was something to be ashamed of.

"What do you do for a living? A writer and editor? Who do you work for? Oh. Yourself? Are you published? Self published? Where can I find your work?"

That was usually the end of it. Everyone wondered but no one bought books or requested services. No answer was good enough for them.

Yes, I was proud of my own accomplishments but everyone around me was so critical that I chose to stay home to work to care for my son. At that point in my life, Bam was everything to me and I knew that I could make it as an entrepreneur.

Not to prove them wrong. But to deafen the echoes of insecurities and self-doubt that I used from their words as an excuse to oppress myself. I made the negativity my own. I hid in it. When I decided to make the choice to stop living an inadequate life, I realized that I was just acting in fear.

After almost losing my business and after my relationship with Doug, I felt paralyzed and couldn't move on. Or was it that I *wouldn't* move because I was afraid to fail again?

What happens when it's test time and you don't take the test? You still get a failing grade. You've wasted needless time and the test you've avoided taking is still going to be there. It's *always* going to be there. You have to face the future and walk in it. Make a conscious decision to avoid pitfalls instead of reacting to what's happening.

What was my role in it all? How can I change the direction of what's happening?

I said to myself, "You are not doing enough in your life and I'm disappointed that you haven't achieved your full potential yet."

Thinking about it made me realize that the real message from the people I called naysayers was all in my own head. Forget about what other may say, that negative self-talk can really get to you. So I spun the message around.

You are so talented. Stop beating yourself up about the past. Pick yourself up and keep pushing through."

Negative thinking derails you. When you become consumed with proving "others" wrong, even that pushes you into doing something against what you want for yourself. Then you end up on a course in the wrong direction. The cycle perpetuates itself within. It kept happening to me.

But I did it to myself. No one else to blame. I think about all of the times that I did things for other people's benefit that I forgot what I wanted for myself. I was afraid to fail in doing what I loved so I immersed myself in other's dreams.

Everything I did brought me to now, but really: Did I need a video gaming lounge? Should I have been an electrician? I did all of these things knowing I love to sing and write. I psyched myself out of my dreams before because despite what others thought, I could make a successful living at what I wanted to do. I just didn't know how yet. Lessons learned:

• Use your own words of encouragement to really listen to yourself, breathe life into yourself so that you can grow out of the storm of your own complacency.

• Listen to yourself. Don't use anyone else's thoughts of what you should do because it would only be based on what would be good to them. You usually know what to do. Trust yourself. I listened to my dad and stayed with

Doug. I didn't listen to myself when I gave Jason my investment money instead of banking on myself. I let other's dreams become my dreams, destroying myself as I followed in their wake instead of trusting myself and making my own way. But what did *I* want?

CHAPTER FIVE :

SAGGY MARTYR

I've always pushed my son towards greatness. I've always wanted to bring out the best in him. But how I could do this if I was hiding behind him?

It occurred to me one day that behind my son was where I felt safe. I could always say, "I'm doing this or that for my son." Instead of I'm doing this for myself.

Who does being a martyr serve? Not me and definitely not my son.

Hiding in mediocrity is cowardice. No one is happy knowing that they're designed for bigger and better things and letting time slide by. What did I want to do with my own life? It wasn't too late for me. What greatness did I want to show my son? He needed to see an example of action, not just saying.

Actions always speak louder than words. I was the only one he could see up close and personal. Everyday. With maximizing my own greatness, I could bring out the best in him.

So I asked myself again, "What did I want?" That's when the lost and sinking feeling set in. I honestly didn't know. I only knew that I could sing great, had imagination to write books and tell stories with messages, great eyesight and a vast vocabulary to edit books, so I figured I'd run with that.

Problem was, I wasn't being totally honest. I was telling half-truths to protect the guilty and spare the perception of "good ol' Birdie" by not even revealing the bad and the ugly about myself. I was tearing at the seams with guilt. And I wanted to be free.

As a child, I sang all of the time, mostly

enjoyable, but my family would hush me once in a while. They were probably tired of me. When in school, sometimes kids would say that I didn't sound good, although that probably came from jealousy, I still began doubting myself. So I started to lip sync in groups of friends. I still loved my voice, in secret.

Years later, when I sang publicly again, everyone loved it and told me how great of a singer I was. But every time I would try out for a play in school, my talent was overlooked because I wasn't popular. The same people got picked for everything. I'd end up like a tree or a silent sidekick. Yes, it hurt.

At that time, I didn't feel like I was enough. I wanted to be a known performer but I was stuck playing the background.

I didn't feel cool enough, pretty enough, smart enough or good enough. While I never compared myself to anyone in particular, I lived my life looking out of a window from the inside, always yearning for more but held back by an invisible force. But I know that I am not the only person that felt that way, so: So what?

In being stuck in those feelings that resonated with me in the past, was I crippling my son, the way that I was?

Did he see my internal conflicts and insecurities and struggle with the message I was sending out with my actions versus the things I had said?

As I got older, I understood. Good enough isn't *good enough*, so why didn't I do more? And now that I understand, why wasn't I doing more now?

It happened. I realized what it was one afternoon.

I had always prided myself on my appearance, vain even. Even after I had Bam, I took pride, even in the stretch marks...

Correction, I accepted them as a part of motherhood. A badge of motherhood. Can't change it, so why fight it?

I was at a party and when I got a hot flash, I went into the coatroom to take off the sweater I was wearing. As I took it off, my blouse that was underneath lifted up and my belly was exposed for like 5 milliseconds; I quickly pulled it down and I looked in the doorway and there was Doug, I saw him glancing at me and his face changed.

It was a look of disgust. To this day, he doesn't remember the instance and in his defense, it was my own insecurities and I'm sure that he didn't mean to hurt me. But I definitely didn't feel good about myself.

In all of the times of my *Saggy Boobs & Stretch Marks exposed life*, I was defined in that moment, now naked and exposed. For the first time in my life, I realized that didn't like myself.

His cheating at the time didn't help that feeling. I felt so unsexy. I always knew that it was him and his own stuff that made him cheat but in that moment, I became a homely mom that was plain and out of shape...

Definitely the real reason why he was cheating, right? No! His stuff wasn't *my* issue. But it was easy for me to justify his actions with self-blame. I wasn't bright and shiny anymore. I was undesirable and was on autopilot and just existing. I was heartbroken, sad and broke.

How twisted I became as I slowly shrunk into a role I never thought I'd play.

That shrinking feeling never went away. Would I ever feel beautiful, loved and sexy ever again?

C'mon we all know the answer to that now. But when you're in it, you're a certified mess. How could you ever see your way out of it?

I was at my lowest and I wanted so bad to be the best mom, best partner, best author, best businesswoman and I was stuck being who I swore I'd never be.

It was like being brand new and then recognizing your version of you is obsolete.

Instead of being able to take pride of being in great working condition and still rare and unique, you've downgraded to bare minimum use as you compare yourself to the new models with the bells and whistles but not seeing the expendability of the newer models because you were actually **built to last.**

The only motivation I had at the time was my son. Getting out of the bed was easier because him getting the best education was my motivation. The best life for him was paramount and I was determined to make it happen. So I started there.

I decided to change my mind as I changed myself. In that moment, life as I knew it had changed. I decided to see the beauty in others. I found the good in others.

All I wanted was others around me to be happy. And they were. It was a way for me to find a skosh of happiness without looking at myself for immediate improvement. I felt invisible, like the stereotypical undesirable from a movie, but in real life and in action.

I was suffocating in the hurt and hate I had for what I felt others did to me. The more I was consumed with getting my money from Jason, losing my love with Doug and obsessed with getting my life back, the more the lack of money, relationships and my life spiraled downward.

The energy you put into that thing magnifies its importance to the blindness of everything else because of the lack of what you want is the only thing you see. That's how you keep losing.

My love life was non-existent and time just passed me by. I didn't really date. I just fell into situationships that turned into relationships that didn't last. I was broken.

I wanted to write my stories and help others reach understanding. How could I do that when I myself didn't understand? I was still stuck under the rubble. The words I needed to say were stuck and I couldn't get them out. The murmurings stung and the gossip pissed me off, then the *"you'll never be anything"* started to be louder.

Months later, I was back to feeling like the nothing I was before. The head start window I gave myself was slowly closing and I was clamoring for it to stay open. It's like those who wait the last minute to do their taxes, or study for tests.

What I failed to realize was that it is always time to set out for what you want to do. It's like jump rope. You wait for the right time to jump in, because there's an opportunity to begin every time the rope turns The rhythm of the rope swing always allows you an in.

Mommies always tell their babies, "You can be whatever you want to be when you grow up. Sky's the limit!"

But he's seeing: Mommy is afraid to take the leap and actually be a grown up. You see what I mean?

We grow up with people telling you what to believe, what you should have faith in, but never do they send you on your way to be equipped for your own journey on finding your own faith and get your own set of ideals and beliefs.

Bam said to me one day, "Mom, I think I'm a Buddhist." I smiled and asked why did he think that way, he said, "If I die, I want to come back as something great." I asked him, "Why would you have to die to become something great?" He could start by being great now and if he died and lived a great life and was a great person, he'd probably be back as something or someone greater. So could I.

Although we aren't Buddhists, why would I ever discourage his thought process by telling him we don't believe in Buddhism or discourage his thoughts about death? I saw it as a moment to shift his thinking in having a good life and being a great person now. "Let's not wait Bam, live your best life now."

Knowing that actions speak louder than words, what can I do today to show him that now is the time for me to be the best me?

One thing that women are conditioned to think about motherhood is that in everything you do, you're always last. The self-sacrificing saving Grace, the martyr.

If you're one of the lucky ones that's got it all figured out, that's cool for you. But if you're still juggling, the important things only get minimum attention. In function mode, doing things just in order to get to the next thing but nothing ever really gets the deeper attention it deserves.

That means you being a mother suffers because you're only scratching the surface on being a mom. On top of that, if you're juggling your health, your business, your love life, it will suffer somehow and you may end up dropping the ball somewhere. I can speak that from experience.

School, work, baby, relationship, my

father's death... But that's wrong. Where am I in the equation?

Which is why I say: YOU CAN'T PUT THE KIDS FIRST! "You can't pour from an empty cup."

Now it s ME, my son, family, his school, expanding my business and love life. Sometimes the order shifts but I have to take care of myself *first*.

There's always going to be something. Ascertain the priority and work your way down the list.

As I got older, I started getting heartburn. The voices, the mental games, other people's issues; became too much for me my chest began to hurt and I started having panic attacks. Being a martyr for everyone else gave me an excuse to not put my own chaos into order. I put their bull in front of me and decided not to deal... My own plate was full, right?

What if I had a heart attack and died? The kids would get fed from someone else, everyone would mope for a while but life goes on. You wouldn't be completely forgotten but you'd definitely be a distant memory.

Why do that to yourself and your family?

Love yourself more. Priorities may change from day to day, but if you're productive and take care of business, it will get done.

But **you** have to come first.

I know it's easier said than done. But it's true. You can't pour from an empty cup. Take care of yourself first.

Or you'll crash and burn.

My mom and I had a deep conversation and at the end, she asked me if I knew what my life's purpose was.

Without thinking about it, effortlessly, I said, "To sow seeds."

"Sow seeds?"

"Yes, Mom. What I say and do is sowing a

seed for someone else. It's important that everything I do has meaning." I can own that honestly.

In owning situations in my own life, I've always been perceptive to the extra stuff in order to circumvent the hard-to-deal with things. But as far as reaching deep, I was still afraid.

When we re younger, we try so hard to make our parents proud. When we're older, we try to keep our children proud. It's uncanny how it shifts. We only have a small window to make it count for ourselves and make ourselves proud.

And in that, we can either propel ourselves to greatness in that window or our children become the reason we shrink back and become martyrs.

We're "sacrificing" or "putting our children first". I thought that I was being noble. The thing is, your child sees you living that half-life and that begins to become what they've accepted. They become conditioned to think that living that half- life is ok for them too.

How can we change that? By living. Really living well and including them on the process. Life is good, but short. Let them enjoy you in your greatness every day. It makes a difference. Success is determined by how many times you get up once knocked down. Why wouldn't I get up and strive to be the best me?

I needed to put that mask back on to start to heal on the inside.

The healing process is an amazing thing. It was like a fractured bone that needed a cast. This hard exterior piece is added to you so that guards the soft, fragile and broken part of you so can heal.

My cast was this book. And the mask I wore everyday was for everyone else that I couldn't share my inner working.

Where was my pride? What did I stand for? What was I doing with my life? I wanted more but I didn't know how to take myself there. I could see the solutions to everyone else's problems and make solutions for them so easily.

My own answers were staring me right in the face but I couldn't read the message yet. Frustrating to say the least. When I looked inward, I found it.

CHAPTER SIX :

SAGGY PERSPECTIVE

In my life, I've been able to make good friends and companions. I'm very friendly by nature, so forming alliances isn't hard for me. A lot of them have turned into lifelong friendships. In choosing companions, I've also noticed that I haven't always been the best judge of character.

With that said, I continue to live by the mantra, "Love like you've never been hurt."

However, I do add on, "No matter what, be true to yourself, take the lesson: people are in your life for reasons, seasons or both. If you hold on longer than you should, you'll both be hurt so pay attention." "Bruised and battered, you still deserve love, don't be afraid to fall." There's more where that came from. But I digress.

Owning your part in the end of a friendship or relationship is so important as a part of the healing process. It's so easy to place blame on someone else when it ends. But realistically, how can you place blame when it takes an active two (minimum) in a relationship or friendship? Again, when you blame each other, you both give up your power to change. I didn't see it then, I was just hurt and was still reeling from what happened with Jason.

Bottom line is: I learned a skill that got me through it.

Forgive, forget and pretend that you got over it... and eventually you will.I didn't say ignore it. I didn't say cover it up.

Yes, I said, forgive, forget and pretend you got over it. Brush off the debris from the wreckage and move on. Still with scars, so it

Success is your best revenge. When you get up, dust yourself off, you can choose to make everyday count is when you become ready to change your own life.

It's like when we tell our kids that are afraid of the dark. I always say, "Think happy thoughts and eventually, you will become happy." Sounds easier said than done. Please understand that I know that it won't minimize your initial pain. But I will say that your pain will only exist as long as you let it.

In the days that I was waiting for my son to get out of school when we were commuting, I've met some great people. My mobile office was either at Whole Foods, the New York Public Library, Central Park and my son's own school. The people I've crossed paths with, have helped me so much along my journey in shaping who I've become. I'm so grateful for them.

To this day, I get so emotional when I state the instances in which those wonderful people had helped me. I usually speak of them in my classes and workshops that when something is meant for you, the way will be made. I have been blessed so much more than I've been hurt. That's the perspective.

We aren't alone on our journeys. We are all at a crossroads when we meet and we are all looking for more. Finding our way hasn't been and won't be easy but we are steadily finding it.

In meeting people, I've been balanced in ways I always needed to be and been helped to see my worth in a lot of situations.

All I hope is that I've been a good enough friend to them as they've been to me. I used to say, "If only I had someone that made my life easier, simplify my life. Encourage me and help me."

I realized that I have that. I've always had that. People that have loved me and wanted what's best for me and have been cheering me on all along when I felt the most alone. I am truly grateful for them.

There are two types of people in pain:

First type, when you ask them how they feel, they say, "Oh, not good. I have my good days but more bad days." They seem to be dwelling and wallowing in the pain and it's depressing to see. Seeing them in action, you wish their pain would go away for them. So you tell them to feel better and wish them well. Keep them in your thoughts, well wishes and prayers.

Then there s the other type. The ones that you know are in pain that always wear a smile and give positive energy anyway. The same people that end up inspiring you or just make you realize that your own pain is not the end of the world. That there's someone out there that has it worse than you do. But there they are, the pillar of strength.

Heard the expression, "Fake it 'til you make it?" In that case, I believe the word fake gets a bad rep.

If you look at the dictionary meaning for the

verb, fake is when you "make (an event) appear to happen" or you "accomplish (a task) by improvising.

Ever have a situation that you had to make a miracle happen? You don't panic, you improvise.

Lemonade out of lemons, right?

So fake it, 'til you make it! Another thing I learned in the struggle to rediscover myself: when you're at your worst, look your best.

Do your hair, clean your house. You will feel better. If you're feeling empty, do things that fill your life. Spend time alone. Or spend time with people that care about you. Do the things that you like to do.

Faking it 'til we make it even counts for forgiveness. Forgiveness has many different phases. Sometimes we realize that we still harbor feelings of resentment. Or you just haven't forgiven completely. Is that wrong? No. We are only human. So we have our moments of weakness. But what are you benefitting from by holding on to the anger and hurt? It serves no one. Not them and definitely not you.

It used to bother me when people would thank their haters. Because I'd rather ignore the people who aren't "pro-me". But I do have an appreciation for them.

When they made circumstances in my life harder than it had to be, it gave me the experiences I needed to get me to this point of realization and growth. So when I say that I wouldn't have been able to do all of this without their deeds, I mean that.

Even if our interaction was just a moment, it changed me. I'm glad that the reason for our season but I'm even more glad that it was temporary and that it ended.

So now what?

Acceptance: I always think of the Serenity Prayer when I think about the things I have no control over.

"Please grant me the serenity to accept the things I cannot change, courage to change the things I

can,and the wisdom to know the difference."

We need those reminders that there are things in this life we will not be able to change. All we can ask for is courage to face it and wisdom to deal with all that it is and all that follows.

CHAPTER SEVEN:

SAGGY ME

After struggling with Miss Birdie's Books, Inc. for many years, I decided that I wasn't going to hide and be ashamed of failing anymore. I sat down and thought really hard to figure out what it was that was holding my business and me back. The ugly truth was: It was me, all me.

I was missing. Who was Birdie Chesson?

I am a mother. Singer/songwriter, publisher, author/illustrator, book and lifestyle coach, public speaker, blogger, creator. A Jane-of-all-trades.

But I am still Shaunna (pronounced Shawn-nay) Chesson, a young girl from Staten

Island that loves to sing and write.

As an adult, I was still so torn behind who everyone wanted me to be, who I knew I was and wanted to become that I wasn't doing a good job being all of the above and being the best mom at the same time.

"Where did **Birdie** come from?" I became Birdie when I was working in the village at an online clothing store called Delia's. There were so many great people that just needed a job and at

the same time on the same uncertain path of finding out who we were and who we were going to be. We made so many memories.

Some nights we would have our own version of "Star Search", where we would rap, sing and even dance. On those nights, I was unafraid and would sing as if my life depended on it until I got comfortable enough to sing all of the time like I did when I was a child. No matter where we were in our lives, we all belonged there.

My friend Fitz, started calling me Songbird,

then Birdarella and finally Birdie. It suited me and stuck.

Birdie was Shaunna Reborn and now I m just Birdie. Period. Unashamed and unafraid. Just like we have the life that we are born into, we can always choose (by living) the life that we want to have. Decide. Choose it. Live it. I had forgotten that free part of me.

There are things that happen in your life that cause you to shift gears closer to who you are supposed to be. I have been fortunate to have many of those opportunities. When my brother Ian and cousins Dean, Will and Egon, who are also artists, decided to make an in-home studio, I was like YES!!

My first album, Scandal was born. I got all of the creative juices circulating again. I was able to sing my own songs, on my own terms. We had all night sessions and made great music. When I released it to the public, of course, no one knew me.

So all I had was the feedback from those who loved me. Now everyone that knows me, knows that I can sing. Like siinnnnngggg!

But to them, I was holding back. They didn't have many kind words for it. At first, I was hurt by the critiques.

Then I remembered that opinions are subjective, and everyone has one, right? For the people that hated it, there were also a lot of people that loved it. In hindsight, maybe I was holding back but making a professional album was foreign to me.

All of my creative juices were finally coming together and into fruition for me. I finally knew what I wanted and I was just going to go for it full blast. I knew that my son was going to be proud of his mama. I was finally on my way again.

I was looking past all of the hurt, heartbreak, failure and denial, but the tax liens and penalties I had racked up all of these years with a failing business finally caught up to me.

So, I got a job. Now there is absolutely nothing wrong with "getting a job" but I hadn't worked for anyone since my electrician days over 10 years ago and was not good at answering to anyone.

But I also knew that with the amount of debt that I had racked up, there was no way that I could dig out by myself. And I needed to connect to the world in another way.

After being a staple in my son's school for several years, I moved on to working in a high school. It was a great job. Something I was very proud of, I was good at it and it was a great place to work. I was a Parent Coordinator in one of the newest, premier public high schools in NYC. We were adults and kids at a crossroads so to speak, from all over needing that extension from home and it was definitely that place.

There, I had a great team, great staff, a true family in a sense. The kids for the most part, loved me and I loved them so much. I was

Miss Birdie to them. They were so smart, full of life and very curious. They'd Google all of the staff and when it came to me, they'd recite my bibliography, sing my music and ask me questions about my career choices. And while I loved my job and still have several lives in many other industries, I was stalled at this point. I literally sought safety from a storm and stayed on the island, even after the rescue.

I took the definition of my job description as defined and made it my own. I thought I was doing a great job; it also started to feel uncomfortable. I was creatively drained. I was living and breathing this job like it was my life, because it became my life. Never mind the fact that this was just supposed to be a means to an end, not a life-long career.

I started having heartburn again, but it seemed to get worse. I was taking Zantac and Prilosec all of the time. Then I would have erratic heartbeats. I thought I was having panic attacks. I didn't think that I was that stressed out but I was falling apart.

I was gritting my teeth at night. The stress was taking a toll on me.

One day, during a fire drill, my heart started to beat so fast that I felt faint. I calmly got the kids back inside and left to go to the hospital. My heart rate was over 200 beats a minute. The doctors came out and took me in. They were trying so hard to get my heartbeat down; it eventually took over an hour. They had to shock my heart 3 times to stop it. It was heart arrhythmia. The realization woke me up and it made me very sad.

The last time I made a huge shift in my life against my better self, I started to have seizures. That was almost 20 years ago when I went to business school as per my mother's wishes instead of following my own dreams. Even your body tells you clues about going against yourself but I didn't listen and took the long way again.

Even after that, I still wasn't ready for the push off the ledge. The wake up call needed to happen somehow. I was slipping away and time waits for no one. I had heart surgery and went back to my job. But I was not all in anymore. I felt like I was wasting away and was miserable.

I wanted more and knew I deserved more but I was definitely lost in the how again. I started to project my frustrations and bitterness. I was scared and angry at myself.

When hermit crabs grow, they get too big and uncomfortable so they need to crawl out of their shell in their most vulnerable and naked state in the search for the shell that actually fits. Which was very indicative of my journey back to myself.

At this stage in my life, I just wanted somewhere to stay dry for a little but it was evident, I was too big and I definitely wasn't meant to work for someone else for much longer. I had to do inventory.

I got home one night and went through the collection of unfinished products that I had racked up: 9 books, 4 TV and movie scripts, a tee- shirt line and revamp of Miss Birdie's

Books, Inc. All of it was waiting for me to finish. Finish. And release it. Let the world know who you are, FINALL Y!

They say that you make time for the things that matter to you, but I was giving no time to the things I said I loved.I was neglecting a whole life that had been waiting for me for so long. I was older than most of my coworkers and was probably the most restless. Not to mention I was now a part-time mom, ordering delivery so that I could work late. I was not happy. Neither was Bam.

In reflection, I started a whole batch of existences to distract myself from the life I was meant to have. People were starting to call me on it again. "What are you up to now?

I was avoiding past think tanks and motivational pontiffs because who likes looking at themselves when they don't like who they're becoming?

I absolutely love myself but as much as I

loved my job, it was totally eclipsing who I was supposed to be, where I was supposed to stay.

This wasn't my stop, this wasn't meant to be what I wanted to do for the rest of my life. And I didn't want to wait until I turned 40 to enjoy my life. My time was now.

I never quit anything before. But I made sure that my work was done and I decided to make my exit. I could not have been in a better place to lose and quickly find myself and I absolutely loved my job and definitely had no regrets in my important position, but I was literally meant to fly higher.

So what now?

For a long time, I believed that I had been trapped in my talents. How could I be so talented and not go far?

My talents: I can sing and my gift is that I have a way with words. Through my gifts and talents, I can show my heart, use my mind and voice to share with the world. I'm transparent, for all to see.

I needed to make those a part of the legacy that I left for my son. But I never seemed to have enough time or mental energy to get anything done. Whenever I did get energy, I'd pounce on it and go marathon style and then burn out.

Intention: all there. Motivation: dead.

What was there left to do? Finish and grow. Let go and release. So I quit my job and decided to go full speed ahead, being the best me I could be.I started talking to myself more. I recorded myself as if I was talking myself into a different perspective. Thank goodness for social media, which gave me the outlet to really talk out loud and share how I felt.

So every morning, after I kissed Bam on the forehead and sent him on the bus to school, I would take a walk to clear my head and post a video. It was mostly ways to motivate myself. Ironically, I don't post most of my videos. I save most of them to remind myself of where I am and notes for my future self.

Both ways, I was slowly shifting myself upwards. That led me back into public speaking. I remember my first speaking engagement after 20 years. I was so nervous and sweaty. When I stepped on to the stage and remembered all of the training that I had in the past with public speaking talks and performing live.

The fear went away in realizing that the people I talked to, the ones that felt inspired by my words were just like me. People that wanted moreout of life or people that just wanted to feel better. I was home and I instantly started to feel better. Like I was finally on the right track. I was feeling restless, like I had outgrown my life again.

So what was my solution? What was I supposed to do? What was next?

Getting ready to be ready for the next stage in my life.

There's nothing like having a clear picture of what is to come for you and deciding to leave behind what others want you to do, have or to be. I started to write this book all over again, cutting and adding to my story. And it's all here for you.

In that process, I realized that I was doing the same thing again and again, feeling the same sadness and the happiness of mini victories that were the roller coaster that became my life. I was just getting older but everything was staying the same.

But did I have to stay the same? I was still the same saggy boobs, stretch marks and saddlebags that I felt I was. But I wanted to be more.I didn't want to be the hiding, martyring and lonely Birdie. The Birdie that was on the outside looking in at the life that me and my son deserved. So why was I continually doing that to myself?

Here's the thing about mediocrity:

Settling into an inadequate life is like living at 50% when you could easily have an attainable 100% life. Sounds silly, right? So why live that way?

Where is being a better you when you're

comfortable with being uncomfortable?

So, I asked myself, am I looking for a medal for all of the suffering in silence when the reason for all of the suffering was all me? After all, it was my choices and me wallowing in the consequences that brought me to my knees.

The vicious cycle was only happening because I didn't want to even look at my failures, let alone learn from them.

Did my struggle justify the journey or did I want my journey to justify my struggle?"

Either way, I didn't want to struggle anymore. So I invested in myself and decided to go after what I wanted: a better life and everything that included. All I needed to do was give myself permission to want more.

Permission to change. So I changed. Ever since then, I haven't looked back. I'm so much happier and definitely more successful.

I make it a point to only do things that I love, have things I want and be around people that feel good to be around. I come from a place of love and appreciation with everything and in that I have found freedom. I love my life.

What I wanted to share with you became easier to share because I wasn't ashamed of my past failures, I was able to look back and not let any of it define or deter me from my future.

I made the decision to become the best Birdie ever. I love you and want the same for you.

THANK YOU

First, I would love to thank my son Bam for being my constant inspiration to be the best mom that he deserves. I love my niece that makes me aware that love always unfolds and because of our unconditional bond, our love grows stronger and stronger. You munchkins make me want to be bigger and better.

Thank you Fitz, for my name. You have no idea the monster you created. I'll always love you.

Doug for giving me our greatest gift.

I would love to let my family know that I love them and I'm always grateful for our journey that's still unfolding, full of love, life and laughs. So much more is to come!

To my siblings: All 4 One!

Thanks to my parents, Buzz and Babs, I love you.

To the wonderful friends that I've met along the way on my journey to myself, *you* are my earth angels. Thank you so much for your abundant kindness and supportive guidance. Your generosity has helped me in ways that you can't even imagine. May everything that you wish for come true. You deserve the love.

To those who have contributed to the contrast of the goodness in my life, I am grateful for the experience in our dealings. I wouldn't understand how blessed I truly am without our dealings. I forgive you.

ABOUT THE AUTHOR

Birdie Chesson is the Author & Publisher for all of her many books of various genres. She also teaches others how to write their own books through her Speaking & Bookcoaching workshops and seminars with over 30 years experience as a public figure. She is the mother of a son, Bam.

To find out more about her, visit: www.BirdieChesson.com